Recipes from Safe Haven Restaurant Allergy & Gut Friendly Food

Penelope Baalman

DEDICATION

This book is dedicated to Andrew, a friend I shared a mutual interest in low-sugar wholefoods with for many years and who directed me to the SCD. And to my father Stuart, who in his 70's embraced low carbohydrate eating and who never let a carcass leave the house without first turning it into stock. He also believed the majority of doctors "didn't have a clue what they were talking about" when it came to most chronic diseases.

CONTENTS

ACKNOWLEDGMENTS

I would like to thank my friends Vicki Alvos and Sharon Toy for their support and encouragement in the writing of this book and more.

INTRODUCTION

This book contains recipes for items sold at Safe Haven Restaurant, plus a few extras. Safe Haven Restaurant was a convenience restaurant that operated in Australia during 2017 in an attempt to make gut-friendly food readily available. The aim was to make low-sugar wholefood tasty and convenient so as to provide a viable alternative to unhealthy options.

There are three main differences between the recipes contained here compared to most similar cookbooks; they were designed to be efficient time-wise, they were designed to use relatively cheap ingredients and they were designed to provide meals and drinks similar to those that could no longer be eaten out and that were sorely missed while improving your health.

In the restaurant it was important to use easy recipes with reasonably low-cost ingredients that could be provided quickly and cheaply so as to be competitive with fast food options. When applied to the home this means meals that can readily be re-heated and mix and matched for variety but do not require making every single meal from scratch every time.

One of the challenges set when developing items was to make vegetable dishes that would be attractive to children and men as generally being harder to convince of the benefits of eating vegetables.

Over the months we operated it was heartening to see how much customers enjoyed the items. Some customers were highly vocal about how great everything tasted including many who did not have any gut, food intolerance or weight issues but simply wanted something quick and healthy yet tasty and satisfying. The phrase "This tastes amazing!" was heard regularly. During the time we were open we only ever got one outcome of star rating from our reviews on Facebook; five stars.

Unfortunately the restaurant did not succeed, not from lack of enthusiasm for the taste of the food but rather financial miscalculation in regards to supporting a restaurant in the first year.

Safe Haven's rules followed those of the Specific Carbohydrate Diet (SCD) and the Gut and Psychology Syndrome (GAPS) and Small Intestinal Bacterial

Overgrowth (SIBO) diets; eliminating certain sugars and starch, yeast, soy and of course processed foods. These diets are essentially the same as the 'Autoimmune paleo' diet that has recently evolved.

The restaurant avoided all grains, yeast, milk, soy, peanuts, fish, poppy seeds, sesame seeds, sunflower seeds and most nuts. We avoided dairy as much as possible. We did use Havarti cheese as an option on some items and crème fraiche (fermented cream) and butter in limited desserts. We only used unrefined pink salt; we did not use vegetable oils for cooking; we did do any high temperature cooking. We only used cold-pressed vegetable oils; restricted to olive oil for dressings and macadamia oil for mayonnaise and desserts. We avoided fruit as much as possible and only used honey and dates as sweetening agents. We only used apple cider vinegar. We were able to source sugar and nitrate free bacon and ham but otherwise only used wholefoods.

The motivation to start a restaurant in an industry with a 90% failure rate was from personal experience of the diet and the realization that I was far from alone in achieving a remarkable improvement in many aspects of health.

I found out I had celiac disease in 2014. While many things improved very quickly soon after giving up gluten I found I was experiencing severe depression for the first time in my life. After some months of confusion it became obvious I would react to even minute amounts of gluten, then dairy, nuts and eggs. I realized I could time it almost to the hour that within ingesting any amount of these foods some 21 hours later depression would begin. As I slowly got better depression turned into anxiety and then irritability if one of these foods were eaten. Eighteen months after starting the diet I never experienced any form of mood disorder again, that was over two years ago now.

My belief is that when you eat a protein your immune system has marked as an enemy that protein makes its way through the damaged intestinal lining and triggers an immune system response. When specific classes of immunoglobulin have finished their function of neutralizing these perceived threats they effectively sit on serotonin receptors while they wait to be absorbed back into the body.

Undoing damage to the intestinal lining and improving the composition of your gut microbiome requires quite strict adherence to this type of diet for likely at least a year, but the benefits are well and truly worth it. I can now eat any of the foods that used to have a terrible effect on me, including even gluten with no undesirable effect at all. I will never make a habit of eating gluten or milk but now enjoy nuts, eggs, cheese and butter.

Even now I continue to gain the benefits of treating my gut properly; effortlessly maintaining a perfect weight and almost never getting a cold or flu amongst others.

CHAPTER 1 BREAKFAST

Initially I found breakfast to be one of the harder adjustments to make. It just seemed strange that it did not revolved around bacon, eggs and toast in some way. Years earlier I stopped ever having cereal but had always found giving up toast with breakfast a step too far for me.

I remember reading one book that discussed how we now have this weird way of thinking of breakfast as being completely differently to the other meals of the day in that it should be so full of grains and sugar. When I first stopped having cereal I realized its true attraction, it is incredibly convenient; quick, easy and cheap.

I now shudder to think that most people start their day with cereal, probably with low fat milk, fruit, fruit juice, toast (often with jam) and a strong coffee with milk and sugar.

I use the rule of no sugar or caffeine to start the day, I think this is a good way to think about breakfast. If you are low on time there are lots of ways to make shortcuts for yourself that still allow you to have a decent meal to start the day. For the most part I would describe my breakfast regime as making good use of leftovers.

Once you start getting used to meat and vegetables for breakfast you really learn to like it. What is especially good is instead of feeling somewhat off afterwards and then hungry within a few hours you feel great to have started the day that way and do not feel the need to eat again until lunch.

I tried not to have the same breakfast within three days. Day one would be self-made sausage patties and cooked tomato (after the first batch of the week they just needed to be re-heated in the oven). The next day I combined curried eggplant and gravy with cottage pie and again all I had to do was re-heat them in the oven so very quick and simple. My consistent favorite was chicken bubble and squeak, your gut definitely thanks you for that start to the day and it tastes really good.

I do occasionally have almond flour pancakes, which can make a nice treat, but I would definitely advise not having this more than once a week at the very most, preferably a lot less, and not until later in the diet. It will also help to break the sugar addiction to avoid such a breakfast as much as possible.

We were able to source nitrate and sugar free bacon. I had one go at making bacon myself, it is actually not that hard, just soaking the appropriate cut of pork in brine for a few days basically. My problem was not having the equipment to slice it thinly. Without the nitrates it also goes that unappealing brown-grey color.

One day I will have another go and will add mashed celery or celery powder to the brine as a natural nitrate and would love to try smoking it too. I do love bacon.

Egg and bacon cups

These are really convenient if you have to take a breakfast with you to eat on the run or to have later as a snack at any time of day. Very tasty. Still works well by leaving the bacon out too, but not as good.

Serves 12

10	Whole	Eggs
6	Rashers	Bacon
2	Cups	Spinach
¼	Cup	Chives, fresh
¼	Cup	Parsley, fresh
1	Teaspoon	Salt
½	Teaspoon	Pepper
½	Teaspoon	Onion powder

Dice bacon and fry on medium heat stirring occasionally and set aside. Line muffin trays with melted bacon fat.

Finely chop spinach, parsley and chives and fry on low to medium heat until softened. Add bacon to pan, mix and then remove from heat.

In a medium mixing bowl add eggs, salt, pepper and onion powder and whisk lightly. Spoon even amounts of spinach, herb and bacon mix into muffin tray and then add egg mix to fill to ¾ full.

Bake at 170°C (340°F) for approximately 20 minutes until egg is cooked.

Breakfast sausage or patty

There are two sausage patty recipes here, the breakfast and a mild Italian type. The breakfast is nice at breakfast time but I never felt it was as good later in the day. I tried my hand at actual sausage making with not great results and the clean-up I found too time consuming. If you like it though by all means make sausages instead, they will not dry out as much and hold their flavour better. But I found if you simply process the ingredients until they start to stick together so they bind and then fry them as patties to be almost as good with much less hassle.

Serves 4

500	Grams	Pork mince
1	Teaspoon	Salt
½	Teaspoon	Sage
¼	Teaspoon	Pepper
¼	Teaspoon	Thyme, dried
¼	Teaspoon	Honey (optional)
1	Dash	Marjoram, dried
1	Dash	Chilli flakes
1	Pinch	Cloves, ground

Place 500 g (1 lb.) of pork mince in processor. Add salt, sage, pepper, thyme, marjoram, chilli flakes and cloves. Process all ingredients until mince starts to stick together. Preferably leave overnight in an airtight container.

Melt dripping in large frying pan on low to medium heat. Roll mince into a ball and halve and repeat twice to get consistent sizes of eight patties of about 60 g (2 oz.) each.

Squash mince balls flat into patties and fry until cooked through, approximately 6 to 8 minutes on each side. Serve two patties with a halved fried tomato and top with mayonnaise or tomato sauce.

Italian sausage or patty

This has remained my favourite sausage, nice in the morning and later in the day. I have found my sister and others seem to have a problem with eating coriander in the morning, she still has not tried it. I prefer to crush the garlic and capsicum in a garlic press and remove the skins (they get added to soup or salad) so you get more flavour and an even distribution as being easier and doesn't need good knife skills.

Serves 4

500	Grams	Pork mince
½	Teaspoon	Red capsicum (pepper)
1	Clove	Garlic
1	Teaspoon	Salt
⅔	Teaspoon	Coriander, ground
⅔	Teaspoon	Pepper

Place 500 g (1 lb.) of pork mince in processor. Crush garlic and capsicum with garlic press removing skins and add to processor with salt, pepper and coriander. Process all ingredients until mince starts to stick together. Preferably leave overnight in an airtight container.

Melt dripping in large frying pan on low to medium heat. Roll mince into a ball and halve and repeat twice to get consistent sizes of eight patties of about 60 g (2 oz.) each.

Squash mince balls flat into patties and fry until cooked through, approximately 6 to 8 minutes on each side. Serve two patties with a halved fried tomato topped with mayonnaise or tomato sauce.

Chicken bubble and squeak

This can be made with any leftover meat. Corned beef is actually the best but is difficult to source without the use of sugar and preservatives. Roast beef is also great. If you have cauliflower mash and leftover meat in the fridge it is quick and easy to whip together. This is definitely the breakfast where both my gut and my taste buds say "well done!"

Serves 1

1	Teaspoon	Dripping
1	Small	Onion
1	Small	Tomato
⅓	Cup	Mashed cauliflower
¼	Cup	Chicken, cooked
¼	Cup	Sauerkraut
½	Teaspoon	Chives, dried
¼	Teaspoon	Celery salt

Melt dripping in small frying pan on low to medium heat. Chop onion into 1 cm (½ in.) pieces and fry on medium heat until glassy. Add 1 cm (½ in.) pieces of chopped tomato and continue to fry until soft.

Add cauliflower mash, sauerkraut, chicken, celery salt and chives to pan and fry for a further 5 minutes until heated through, stirring occasionally. Season with extra celery salt to taste.

Cottage pie and eggplant

This was one of my main three breakfasts for a long time. It came about as I had started having re-heated cottage pie for breakfast but realised I didn't have enough for a decent meal one morning. I did have plenty of curried eggplant and gravy though so added that to make a full-sized meal. I found it ten times better than the cottage pie alone. Friends were quite horrified at the concept of this for breakfast, until they tried it.

Serves 1

½	Cup	**Curried eggplant & gravy**
1	Cup	**Cottage pie**

Bake for 15 to 20 minutes at 150°C (300°F) until heated through. Serve with tomato sauce.

Fancy bubble and squeak

We trialled this as a special where initially it was a bit strange looking but the first time the staff tried it (sharing a plate) with each bite those sharing stopped talking and became quicker and quicker in eating to make sure they got as much as possible. We advised customers not to share this meal.

Serves 4

½	Head	Cauliflower
4	Rashes	Bacon
1	Whole	Sugar loaf cabbage
1	Whole	Purple onion
½	Teaspoon	Salt
¼	Teaspoon	Pepper
¼	Teaspoon	Chives
4	Whole	Eggs

Cut cauliflower into small florets and boil in medium saucepan for 3 minutes then set aside. Chop bacon into 2.5 cm (1 in.) pieces and fry on low to medium heat in large frying pan until lightly cooked and set aside.

Thinly slice onion and cabbage and fry in same pan until softened. Add cauliflower and fry for a further 2 minutes. Add bacon, salt, pepper and chives to pan and mix well.

Serve on plate topped with a fried egg.

Hazelnut and almond banana pancakes

At the restaurant we used half hazelnut flour to get that nice taste and half almond flour which is both cheaper and I find sticks together slightly better. Take care when turning as they will not stick together like normal pancakes. Being smaller than standard in size will help them not fall apart when flipping.

Serves 2

2	Whole	Eggs
1	Whole	Banana
¼	Cup	Macadamia oil
½	Teaspoon	Vanilla extract
⅓	Cup	Almond flour
⅓	Cup	Hazelnut flour
½	Teaspoon	Cinnamon
¼	Teaspoon	Bicarbonate of soda
1	Pinch	Salt

In a mixing bowl combine eggs, cut banana, macadamia oil and vanilla and mix well with stick blender.

Mix almond and hazelnut flour with cinnamon, bicarbonate of soda and salt and then blend with wet mix.

Fry small pancakes on low to medium heat flipping when air bubbles appear. Serve with honey and either butter or French cream mix. Can garnish with fried banana slices and swish of honey.

Scrambled omelette

This recipe uses the ingredients for an omelette allowing vegetables and a more interesting taste but is more easily cooked as scrambled eggs. The reason we had this over an omelette was it held better and was readily eaten with just a fork but it also saves time and has a consistent outcome regardless of equipment and skill.

Serves 1

3	Whole	Eggs
1	Small	Tomato
1	Whole	Green onion (shallots)
½	Teaspoon	Salt
¼	Teaspoon	Pepper
½	Teaspoon	Oregano, dried
1	Teaspoon	Dripping

Melt dripping in frying pan on low to medium heat. Finely chop shallots and tomato and fry for 2 to 3 minutes until just softening.

In a small mixing bowl add eggs, salt, pepper and oregano and whisk lightly. Add egg mix to pan and fry for 3 to 5 minutes stirring regularly until cooked. Great with fried tomato and sausage.

Slow cooked scrambled eggs

This was not from the restaurant but my dad's recipe. He was quite inventive as a cook and this was easily my favourite breakfast. The real difference is in the very slow cooking, my father was more patient than I am and he took at least 20 minutes. The main thing is to serve before either the whites go completely white or the yolks harden fully, so make sure the eggs are fresh and well sourced. I have to admit though it really is better with toast. Now that I am better I have this every month or so with gluten-free bread.

Serves 1

½	Rasher	Bacon (or ham)
3	Whole	Eggs
¼	Teaspoon	Salt
1	Teaspoon	Parsley, fresh

Finely dice bacon and fry on low to medium heat in small saucepan until crispy, stirring and tossing occasionally. Separate egg yolks from whites. Remove bacon and turn heat down to lowest setting. Add egg whites to saucepan and cook very slowly stirring occasionally.

When egg whites are just starting to turn white add yolks, bacon and salt. Continue to cook on very low heat stirring occasionally. Add chopped parsley with a few minutes to go and cook until yolks and whites are just lightly cooked.

CHAPTER 2 VEGETABLES & SIDES DISHES

One of the main challengers of the restaurant was to provide vegetable items that would appeal in taste to everyone, even children. We were also avoiding sugar if at all possible or using the least amount of honey. The other two ways to provide taste other than sweetening is to use fat and salt.

We never cooked with vegetable oils and tried to avoid dairy as much as possible and so used dripping with many dishes. I do firmly believe that decent forms of saturated fat and decent unrefined salt do not represent a health problem. Highly refined industrial salt yes. Heat, chemical and high-pressure extracted vegetable oils yes. Unrefined or low refined forms of fat and salt no.

The habit of reducing fat (especially saturated fat) and salt has become so ingrained now it can be difficult to overcome. This has been such a disaster with processed foods where to make up the taste from their removal even more of the most horrible forms of sugar and flavor enhancing chemicals are added instead. I also avoid vegetable oils high in polyunsaturated fats.

I advise not being scared of unrefined fats used at the right temperatures and using decent salts. Of the recipes that follow I would suggest having the cauliflower mash and carrot mash available in the fridge at all times. I make batches of a size I know will last me for 3 to 4 days. You then have your meal base ready to go to save time.

I would also advise trying the curried eggplant and gravy recipe, it really is very nice and goes well with roast chicken. It also goes really well with any lamb dish alongside fried cauliflower mash. I do recommend trying that as soon as possible.

There is one recipe here which does not meet the rules of the diets as it includes potato. It is easily my favorite potato salad recipe and one few people outside of Germany and Austria know. The ingredients it uses makes it the most healthful form of potato salad I know of. Plus it just tastes really good.

Many of the recipes use dripping where butter could be used instead.

Mashed cauliflower

This basic recipe is easy to make and very versatile when you are avoiding grains and starch. It replaces rice and mashed potato really well and to some extent can be used instead of pasta too if you find yourself without any zucchini. The first cottage pie I made for a friend using cauliflower mash instead of potato mash she had no idea it wasn't potato. I have a batch of this in the fridge at all times ready to go with any number of meals.

Serves 8

1	Head	Cauliflower
2	Tablespoons	Dripping
1	Teaspoon	Salt

Cut cauliflower into large florets and boil in large saucepan until pierces easily with a fork - approximately 10 to 15 minutes. Strain in colander, allow to cool a little and mash with stick blender.

Reduce saucepan to low heat and add dripping. Once dripping is melted add mashed cauliflower and salt and mix well, cooking for 3 minutes. Add additional salt to taste. If mash is overly mushy cook for longer to reduce the water content.

Mashed carrot and chives

This is a nice tasty side to meat meals and also makes for a ready to go base for soup. I also have a batch of this in the fridge at all times so I can readily have a tasty soup at least once a day if not more.

Serves 6

8	Whole	Carrots
2	Tablespoons	Dripping
2	Cloves	Garlic
1	Tablespoon	Chives, fresh
1	Teaspoon	Salt

Peel, top and halve carrots both length and crosswise and add to boiling water in medium saucepan. Cook until pierces easily with fork - approximately 15 to 20 minutes. Peel and crush garlic and chop chives. Strain carrots in colander.

Reduce saucepan to low heat and add dripping, once dripping is melted add garlic and fry for 30 seconds until just softening. Take care not to over-cook.

Mash carrots with stick blender and add to saucepan. Add chives and salt and cook for 3 more minutes mixing well. Add additional salt to taste.

Lightly pickled vegetables

This is a great option to take with you if you are eating away from home and want a salad that will keep well without wilting and is fine without refrigeration for a few hours. I would also take this and some brie to friends places for nibbles.

Serves 6

2	Whole	Carrots
1	Whole	Cucumber
½	Bunch	Radishes
½	Cup	Apple cider vinegar
½	Cup	Water
1	Tablespoon	Honey (optional)
1	Teaspoon	Salt

Peel and top carrots. Quarter and cut carrot and cucumber into 2.5 cm (1 in.) long slivers. Coat with salt and refrigerate for 4 hours.

Sterilise a large jar with boiling water. Bring vinegar and water to boil and allow to cool. If using honey add to vinegar mix after taking off heat and stir in. Strain vegetables and add to jar. Pour vinegar mix to cover and store in the refrigerator overnight.

Vegetable bubble and squeak

This is the same as the chicken bubble and squeak recipe found in the breakfast section without the meat. I find this is a great side to either any pork dish or sausages instead of having a bread roll.

Serves 1

1	Teaspoon	Dripping
1	Small	Onion
1	Small	Tomato
⅓	Cup	Mashed cauliflower
¼	Cup	Sauerkraut
½	Teaspoon	Chives, dried
¼	Teaspoon	Celery salt

Melt dripping in small frying pan on low to medium heat. Chop onion into 1 cm (½ in.) pieces and fry on medium heat until glassy. Add 1 cm (½ in.) pieces of chopped tomato to frying pan and continue to fry until soft.

Add cauliflower mash, sauerkraut, celery salt and chives to pan and fry for a further 5 minutes until heated through, stirring occasionally. Season with extra celery salt to taste.

Curried eggplant and gravy

This recipe is adapted from Raman Prasad's Recipes for the Specific Carbohydrate Diet. My sister always makes sure I have this ready before she comes to visit. It has become a favourite of many a person who had never tried or never liked eggplant before. You need to have chicken pan drippings or gravy saved from your last roast chicken.

Serves 8

2	Large	Eggplants
2	Teaspoons	Salt
2	Tablespoons	Dripping
1	Large	Onion
4	Cloves	Garlic
2	Teaspoons	Cumin ground
1	Teaspoon	Coriander ground
1	Teaspoon	Curry powder
2	Teaspoons	Salt
1	Dash	Cayenne powder
2	Whole	Tomatoes
½	Cup	Chicken pan drippings (or onion gravy)

Slice eggplant 2 to 3 mm (⅛ in.) thick and rub salt into each slice. Line slices upright in a colander and leave for 1 to 2 hours. Drain and pat dry each slice and halve if medium or quarter if large. Measure out cumin, coriander, curry powder and cayenne pepper.

Melt dripping in large frying pan on low to medium heat. Chop onion and add to pan stirring regularly until soft. Add crushed garlic and stir until just softened - do not allow to burn.

Add spices stirring for one minute. Add eggplant and chopped tomatoes. Fry stirring occasionally for approximately 30 minutes until eggplant has lost its mushiness but before it starts to burn.

Reduce to low heat and add chicken pan drippings and 1 teaspoon of salt and cook for approximately 10 more minutes to reduce, stirring occasionally. Add additional salt to taste.

Mashed cauliflower and gravy

This is simply an alternative to mashed potato and gravy as a side. It was one of our many vegetable side dishes available at the shop that was quite popular.

Serves 1

| ½ | Cup | Mashed cauliflower |
| 2 | Tablespoons | Gravy (onion) |

Heat gravy in small saucepan on low to medium heat stirring occasionally. Fry mashed cauliflower in frying pan stirring occasionally until heated through and starting to brown. Pour gravy over cauliflower mash.

Cauliflower Poutine

I lived in Canada for a while where I came across Poutine. It's basically chips and gravy with melted cheese thrown in for good measure. A common dish for those heading home after a long night out. I don't recommend having this every day but it makes for a normalising occasional comfort food.

Serves 1

½	Cup	Mashed cauliflower
2	Tablespoons	Gravy (onion)
2	Tablespoons	Havarti cheese

Heat gravy in small saucepan on low heat stirring occasionally. Fry mashed cauliflower in frying pan on low to medium heat stirring occasionally until heated through and starting to brown. Coarsely grate cheese. Top cauliflower mash with grated cheese and then gravy.

Fleischsalat

The staff found this hard to pronounce and had never heard of it but definitely liked it. The ratio of ham to gherkin can be anything from that below to equal amounts. I rarely measure anything out but just keep adding and tasting until I am happy. If you have a problem with dairy it is also fine with just mayonnaise and no sour cream. I first came across it while living in Germany the day after attending Oktoberfest. It was an absolutely perfect lunch that day.

Serves 4

1	Cup	Ham
4	Whole	Gherkins
½	Cup	Mayonnaise
2	Tablespoons	Crème fraiche or sour cream (optional)
½	Teaspoon	Salt
¼	Teaspoon	Pepper

Slice ham and gherkins into 2.5 cm (1 in.) long and 6 mm x 6 mm (¼ x ¼ in.) wide pieces. Add mayonnaise, sour cream, salt and pepper and mix well with large spoon. Add additional salt and pepper to taste and refrigerate for 30 minutes before eating.

Zucchini noodles

The first time I ever made zucchini noodles I was extremely sceptical that they could replace pasta. I was surprised to find I actually preferred the taste, I was amazed at what a good substitute it was. If using a spiralizer I like to cut across in places to make it easier to eat as it can come out in one very long continuous piece.

Serves 4

8	Whole	Zucchini
2	Tablespoons	Dripping
1	Teaspoon	Salt

Place baking tray in oven and heat to 100°C (210°F). Peel and remove tops of zucchinis. Use either a vegetable spiralizer or a peeler and skewer to make strips of zucchini.

Remove tray and add dripping and allow to melt and cover tray evenly. Evenly distribute zucchini strips on tray and bake for 20 minutes.

Remove tray and add second tablespoon of dripping and salt and mix well.

Carrot fries

We decided to try making carrot fries to add as a special one day to go with our burger wraps. When we pulled out the first trial batch I was sceptical that they would sell or go down that well but the staff sea-gulled them terribly and they were gone in seconds. Bake for less if you like soft fries and longer if you prefer crispy fries.

Serves 4

6	Whole	Carrots
2	Teaspoons	Celery salt
2	Tablespoons	Dripping

Place tray in oven and preheat to 200°C (390°F). Peel, top and cut carrots into French fry-sized pieces.

Remove tray and add dripping and allow to melt. Add fries and 1 teaspoon of celery salt and toss to cover. Bake for 20 minutes and remove and toss with second teaspoon of celery salt.

Austrian/Bavarian potato salad

This is of course not legal while on the diet. Once I was better I did start having it once or twice a year though. I also made this for our final staff lunch and it was gone before I got any. The pickled garlic was an idea of my cousin's and is optional but really improves it. Variations are adding ½ cup heated meat broth when combining potato with vinegar and lightly frying onion first. Using Kipfler potatoes is a must.

Serves 8

1	Kilogram	Kipfler potatoes
1	Large	Onion
⅓	Cup	Apple cider vinegar
1	Teaspoon	Pickled garlic (optional)
1	Teaspoon	Salt
¼	Teaspoon	Pepper
4	Tablespoons	Avocado oil
1	Tablespoon	Chives

Place a steaming pot on saucepan half-filled with water and bring to a slow boil. Add 1 kg (2 lb.) of washed potatoes to steamer and cook for 30 to 45 minutes depending on size. Finely dice onion and garlic and mix vinegar with salt and pepper.

Test potatoes after 30 minutes with fork until pierces easily. Remove potatoes from steamer and peel immediately and slice about 4 mm (⅛ in.) thin. Place potato slices in bowl and add onion, garlic, vinegar, salt and pepper. Add a tablespoon of vinegar from the pickled garlic if possible.

Cover bowl with tea towel and leave in sun or warm spot for 2 hours. Add oil and finely chopped chives and any additional vinegar, salt and pepper to taste. Store in refrigerator but serve at room temperature.

CHAPTER 3 MAINS

Main meals revolve around meat and vegetables and are quite normal except that they never include bread, rice, pasta or potatoes but instead use lettuce leaves, cauliflower and zucchini.

Roast dinners are a great way to give yourself cold cuts for the rest of the week for both lunches and other combined baked meals. Chickens are especially useful as they provide you with the carcass for making stock as well as pan drippings for gravy and other recipes.

The following recipes include both those that are really efficient in allowing you to use them again, especially in lunches, and a variety of individual fresh meals for when you have more time.

I would suggest that planning to have a roast chicken every week is a must when on the diet.

Our best seller at the restaurant was easily the chicken fillet wrap, I was quite happy with how that turned out and was received. The chicken garam masala also sold well. The chicken thigh special had some initial skepticism from staff but if it had been on the menu from the start I think it could well have outperformed the chicken wrap.

There are a few recipes here that were not included in the restaurant. This includes the seafood recipes which were problematic in a number of ways and would have added an additional allergen type. I always wanted to add the shish tawook as a special but we never got around to it. I made it for the final staff lunch where it was very well received indeed.

I do not think you have to have huge amounts of meat for every meal, for me about 120 g (4½ oz.) of meat or protein felt about right. At breakfast I did find a higher proportion of vegetables to meat seemed better.

I strongly believe the more your diet consists of just meat and vegetables the easier it is to lose weight. Every now and then I do a couple of weeks entirely sugar free. This means my meals only consist of meat and low starch vegetables.

You really realize how addictive sugar is, even when only consumed in small, natural and simple forms when you do this. It is really quite amazing how body fat is just gone every morning you wake up. Hard to keep going indefinitely but doing this for as many weeks as you can stand will help with both resetting sugar loving gut bacteria to appropriate proportions and breaking the sugar addiction. Without achieving these losing weight is an uphill battle where very few succeed.

Roast chicken

This is an obvious recipe but we did have customers come in and say that our roast chickens were the best they had ever had. The rub does make a difference I think. I always baste my chickens to get the skin crispy as being one of the best bits with all that great fat! I would suggest that this is a meal you make every week as it just goes so far. Most important is getting into the habit of pulling it apart once it has cooled a little to be turned into stock. Make sure you include the legs and wings as they contain some of the best bits. Goes very well with mashed carrot and chives and curried eggplant and gravy.

Serves 4 to 6

1	**Whole**	**Chicken**
2	**Teaspoons**	**Chicken rub**
½	**Teaspoon**	**Salt**
1	**Tablespoon**	**Dripping**

Place tray in oven and preheat to 200°C (340°F). Remove tray and add dripping and allow to melt. Place chicken on tray turning to get dripping coated on skin. First underside shake salt and chicken rub all over, rubbing in with hands, then turn over and do top side (legs in the air).

After 45 minutes turn oven down to 190°C (375°F) and add any vegetables and baste chicken with pan juices. Cook for total of 30 minutes per kilogram but test to be sure it is cooked through.

To test cut thigh and ensure juices run clear and the inner thigh has no pink.

Chicken soup

I believe this to be the single most important and nutritious meal contained in this book. Having a meat broth soup every day I consider to be the most important part of doing the diet. I had three a day to start, then two, and when better one soup every day for three years. During that entire time I never got a single cold (I would normal have two or three a year). Within 6 weeks of only having it occasionally I got my first cold. What I like about this approach of adding pre-made carrot mash from the fridge is it is so quick and easy to put together.

Serves 1

1	Cup	Chicken stock
⅓	Cup	Mashed carrot and chives
¼	Cup	Chicken, cooked
¼	Teaspoon	Salt
1	Dash	Turmeric, ground
1	Pinch	Smoked paprika
1	Pinch	Pepper
1	Clove	Garlic (optional)
¼	Cup	Sauerkraut

Add stock, mashed carrot, salt, turmeric, smoked paprika and pepper to a small saucepan on a low to medium heat.

Squash and pull apart garlic and add to saucepan. Cut chicken into bite-sized pieces and add to saucepan slowly bringing to the boil.

Add sauerkraut to the bottom of a soup bowl. Once lightly boiling pour into bowl.

Chicken garam masala

This was our second best seller and best seller in the cooler months. In our final week we had a bit of a problem for service as a number of customers were coming in and buying the entire tray. You can also use leftover cooked chicken instead of cooking thighs. I would often use the pulp left over from making the ginger drink mix, which was already grated and ready and provided a more subtle ginger flavour I preferred.

Serves 4

2	Cups	Mashed cauliflower
4	Whole	Boneless chicken thighs
1	Whole	Onion
1	Whole	Red capsicum (pepper)
3	Leaves	Spinach
¼	Cup	Chicken stock
1	Whole	Red chilli
1	Clove	Garlic
1	Teaspoon	Ginger
1	Teaspoon	Celery salt
1	Teaspoon	Salt
¼	Teaspoon	Pepper
¼	Teaspoon	Garam masala
2	Tablespoons	Dripping

Make or heat cauliflower mash. If re-heating mash, fry in small frying pan until brown.

Cut chicken thighs into large bite-sized pieces. Chop onion, capsicum and spinach into 2.5 cm (1 in.) pieces. Finely chop garlic and ginger. Add dripping to large frying pan on low to medium heat and cook chicken thighs for 10 minutes stirring and tossing regularly until brown and set aside. Add onion and garlic to frying pan and cook for about 4 minutes until soft. Add chilli and ginger and cook for further 2 minutes.

Add salt, pepper, celery salt, garam masala, stock and chicken and fry until reduced, approximately 5 minutes. Add capsicum and cook for 2 minutes, then add spinach and cook for further 2 more minutes. Serve on hot cauliflower mash.

Australian cottage pie

This recipe came about as a means of having something that filled the loss from not having the occasional Aussie meat pie any more. I made many attempts to make a standard pastry individual pie using both butter and lard pastry with almond flour but never liked the taste of almond flour pastry for savoury dishes. Instead I found making a cottage pie with an Australian meat pie twist was a better alternative. It does require having onion gravy, tomato sauce and Worcestershire sauce ready.

Serves 6

1	Head	Cauliflower
2	Tablespoons	Dripping
1	Teaspoon	Salt
1	Tablespoon	Dripping
500	Grams	Beef mince
½	Cup	Onion gravy
3	Tablespoons	Worcestershire sauce
3	Tablespoons	Tomato sauce
½	Teaspoon	Salt
½	Teaspoon	Pepper

Cut cauliflower into florets and boil in large saucepan until pierces easily with a fork - approximately 10 to 15 minutes. Strain in colander and mash cauliflower with stick blender. Reduce saucepan to low heat and add dripping. Once dripping is melted add cauliflower and salt. Add more salt to taste. Leave aside.

Add dripping to large frying pan on medium heat. Once melted add 500 g (1 lb.) beef mince, cutting and tossing with wooden spoon or spatula to keep separating the mince as soon as it is added. It is important to be attentive at this stage to make sure the mince does not stick together.

Fry for approximately 6 minutes until browned. Add gravy, Worcestershire sauce, tomato sauce, salt and pepper. Bring to the boil and then simmer for 10 minutes. Place in baking pan and top with cauliflower mash and bake at 170°C (340°F) for 20 minutes or until just starting to brown. Serve with tomato sauce.

Cheese burger wrap

This is an easy and basic equivalent of a cheeseburger, but one that doesn't leave you feeling off or guilty at the end.

Serves 4

Patty

500	Grams	Beef mince
½	Teaspoon	Salt
½	Teaspoon	Pepper
1	Teaspoon	Dripping

Per serve

1	Leaf	Lettuce
1	Tablespoon	Onion
½	Whole	Gherkin
1	Slice	Havarti cheese
2	Teaspoons	Tomato sauce
1	Teaspoon	Mustard

Mix 500 g (1 lb.) beef mince in processor with salt and pepper until it just starts to cling together.

Melt dripping in frying pan on low to medium heat and quarter mince, flatten and add patties. Cook on first side for 3 to 4 minutes until brown and flip and cook for a further 5 minutes until cooked through.

Place patty on lettuce leaf as soon as cooked and immediately add sliced Havarti cheese, then mustard, followed by finely diced onion, sliced gherkins and drizzle of tomato sauce.

Sausage, cauli and gravy

This was quite popular with men and older people. It is really a bangers and mash equivalent that was easy to eat without needing a knife, fork and plate.

Serves 1

1	Teaspoon	Dripping
1	Large	Sausage or sausage patty
½	Cup	Mashed cauliflower
¼	Cup	Gravy (onion)

Melt dripping in frying pan on low to medium heat and fry sausages or patties until cooked through, approximately 6 to 8 minutes on each side.

Heat mashed cauliflower in small frying pan on low to medium heat until starting to brown.

Heat gravy slowly on low heat in small saucepan stirring occasionally.

Cut sausage or patty into 2.5 cm (1 in.) pieces and place on mashed cauliflower then add gravy.

Sausage and onion on cauli

This was surprisingly popular, especially with men. It's really a means of having something like a sausage sandwich or roll, substituting for the bread.

Serves 2

1	Teaspoon	Dripping
2	Large	Sausages or sausage patties
1	Cup	Mashed cauliflower
1	Whole	Onion
4	Tablespoons	Havarti cheese (optional)
4	Tablespoons	Tomato sauce

Melt dripping in frying pan on low to medium heat and fry sausages or patties until cooked through, approximately 6 to 8 minutes on each side. Chop onion into thin slices and add to pan after 5 minutes, tossing occasionally.

Heat mashed cauliflower in small frying pan until starting to brown. Cut sausage or patty into 2.5 cm (1 in.) pieces. Place on hot mashed cauliflower and add fried onion and top with cheese and tomato sauce.

Mongolian lamb

Without the flour and cornflour this lacks the thick sauce normal to a Mongolian lamb but I think retains all the flavour. When I got better I started using green banana flour to thicken it and get a more authentic consistency but I wouldn't advise this while on the diet.
Serves 4

500	Grams	Lamb
¼	Cup	Apple cider vinegar
2	Tablespoons	Cauliflower powder
1	Tablespoon	Dripping
1	Large	Onion
2	Cloves	Garlic
1	Tablespoon	Ginger
2	Whole	Green capsicum (pepper)
¼	Cup	Chicken stock
½	Teaspoon	Celery salt
2	Cups	Cauliflower mash

Make or warm mashed cauliflower. If re-heating mash, fry in small frying pan until heated through and starting to brown.

Cut 500 g (1 lb.) lamb into thin strips about 4 cm (1½ in.) long. Mix vinegar and cauliflower powder, pour over lamb and refrigerate for at least 30 minutes.

Add dripping to large frying pan on low to medium heat. Drain off vinegar and add lamb to pan and cook until brown, stirring and tossing occasionally and set aside.

Fry thinly sliced onions for 2 minutes and add crushed garlic and finely diced ginger and fry for a further 1 minute. Add capsicum cut into 2.5 cm (1 in.) pieces and fry for further 2 minutes. Add lamb, stock and celery salt and cook for a final 3 minutes. Serve on bed of hot cauliflower mash.

Chicken salad

*Once I learnt to make a decent mayonnaise and nice salad dressing this became and has remained a favourite of mine. It was my sister who first put me on to the fact that having both salad dressing **and** mayonnaise really makes a salad better. Most days my lunch is either this or chicken soup, more salad in summer and more soup in winter. I have always found that it really benefits from the shallots. I grate extra carrot when making carrot cake muffins and keep it in the fridge so it can be easily added to the salad.*

Serves 1

2	Leaves	Lettuce
2	Small	Tomatoes
1	Tablespoon	Carrot
1	Whole	Green onion (shallot)
¼	Cup	Havarti cheese
4	Whole	Kalamata olives, pitted
¼	Cup	Chicken, cooked
2	Teaspoons	Mayonnaise
3	Tablespoons	Italian salad dressing

Rip lettuce and place in salad bowl. Add chopped tomato, sliced shallots and grated carrot. Add chicken cut into small bite-sized pieces. Add small cubes of Havarti cheese, sliced olives, mayonnaise and salad dressing and toss well.

Sausage salad

When I didn't have any chicken for my normal salad one day I decided to heat up a leftover sausage so that it would taste better and could melt into the cheese for a salad. I didn't actually hold out great expectations but was pleasantly surprised. Some people seem to find the concept weird though.

Serves 1

2	Leaves	Lettuce
2	Small	Tomatoes
1	Tablespoon	Carrot
1	Whole	Green onion (shallot)
¼	Cup	Havarti cheese
4	Whole	Kalamata olives
1	Large	Sausage, cooked
2	Teaspoons	Mayonnaise
3	Tablespoons	Italian salad dressing

Rip lettuce and place in salad bowl. Add chopped tomato, sliced shallots and grated carrot. Add sausage (either hot or cold) cut into small bite-sized pieces. Add small cubes of Havarti cheese, sliced olives, mayonnaise and salad dressing and toss well.

Sausage lettuce wrap

This was supposed to be the substitute for a burger but using a sausage that would both wrap better than a meat patty and hold better.

Serves 1

1	Large	Sausage
1	Leaf	Lettuce
⅓	Whole	Tomato
1	Slice	Havarti cheese
2	Teaspoons	Tomato sauce

Take whole large lettuce leaf and place thinly sliced tomato in middle. Add sausage and top with slice or grated cheese and drizzle with tomato sauce. Wrap lettuce leaf around at base and sides. Can also add thinly sliced onion.

Tip: To harvest the large lettuce leaves for wrapping remove any wilted outer leaves and core the lettuce, then while holding it under running water slowly pull the larger outer leaves off. The water helps immensely in separating the leaves without tearing. Leave the inner section too small for wraps for use in salads.

You can also search the internet for using squares of parchment paper to hold a lettuce wrap in place better or for longer periods like a kebab. It is best to watch a video showing each step.

Coated chicken fillet

The coated chicken fillet was originally made for just the lettuce wraps. As it became cooler we started also using it in a special with hot vegetable sides a bit like a Weiner schnitzel meal.

Serves 4

4	Whole	Chicken thigh, boneless
8	Teaspoons	Chicken fillet coating
1	Tablespoon	Dripping

Add dripping to large frying pan on medium to high heat. Shake chicken fillet coating over both sides of thigh to cover well. Sear fillet on both sides until brown. Turn heat down to medium, cover pan with lid and cook for approximately 8 minutes on each side. Thighs are cooked when there is no pink in the centre or reaches an internal temperature of 165°C (330°F).

Chicken fillet lettuce wrap

Our best-selling meal. I spent some time trying to come up with an alternative to a chicken fillet burger, which I used to love. The coating was the main bit really but the use of thighs suggested by the chefs and cooks worked really well. It is also nice with the addition of a thin slice of ham.

Serves 1

1	Whole	Coated chicken fillet
1	Leaf	Lettuce
⅓	Whole	Tomato
1	Tablespoon	Carrot
1	Slice	Havarti cheese (optional)
2	Teaspoons	Mayonnaise

Take whole large lettuce leaf and place thinly sliced tomato and grated carrot in the middle. Place coated chicken fillet on top with slice or grated cheese and drizzle with mayonnaise. Wrap lettuce leaf around at base and sides.

Coated chicken thigh with carrot and eggplant

There was initially some scepticism about this as a special but it immediately became a best seller. To some extent it replaced the chicken fillet wrap or chicken salad in the cooler months.

Serves 1

1	Whole	Chicken thigh, boneless
2	Teaspoons	Chicken fillet coating
1	Tablespoon	Dripping
⅓	Cup	Curried eggplant & gravy
⅓	Cup	Mashed carrot & chives
2	Tablespoons	Gravy (onion)
1	Tablespoon	Mayonnaise

Add dripping to large frying pan on medium to high heat. Shake chicken fillet coating over both sides of thigh to cover well. Sear fillet on both sides until brown.

Turn heat down to medium, cover pan with lid and cook for approximately 8 minutes on each side. Thighs are cooked when there is no pink in the centre.

Heat gravy, curried eggplant and gravy and mashed carrot and chives in separate saucepans on low to medium heat for approximately 10 minutes each until hot.

Place chicken fillet on plate with eggplant and gravy and carrot on the side. Top chicken fillet with drizzle of mayonnaise and gravy.

Burger patty

This is the basis for the smaller and larger or take-away or sit-down 'burger' options that follow.

Serves 4 to 5

500	Grams	Beef mince
1	Whole	Onion
1	Clove	Garlic
3	Teaspoons	Mustard
2	Teaspoons	Celery salt
1	Teaspoon	Thyme dried
1	Teaspoon	Chives
¼	Teaspoon	Cayenne pepper

Fry diced onion and garlic in pan on low temperature. Let cool to room temperature and add mustard, celery salt, thyme, chives and cayenne pepper.

In a large mixing bowl add to 500 g (1 lb.) beef mince and massage in with hands.

Burger wrap

We put this up as a special one week and it stayed on the menu from then onwards. It did create problems for us timing-wise as the patties did not hold well and needed to be made to order meaning slow delivery. But the response was worth the hassle.

Serves 1

1	Teaspoon	Dripping
1	Large	Burger patty
1	Leaf	Lettuce
⅓	Whole	Tomato
1	Tablespoon	Onion
1	Slice	Havarti cheese
1	Tablespoon	Tomato sauce
1	Tablespoon	Burger sauce

Melt dripping in pan on low to medium heat and fry 120 g (4 oz.) burger patty for approximately 6 minutes on each side until cooked through.

Place sliced tomato and diced onion on lettuce leaf, then patty followed by sliced cheese and drizzle with tomato and burger sauce. Wrap leaf at sides and bottom.

Burger stack

This is essentially the same as the burger wrap but had a larger meat portion and was served on a plate to be eaten with a knife and fork.

Serves 1

1	Teaspoon	Dripping
180	Grams	Burger patty
⅓	Whole	Tomato
1½	Tablespoons	Onion
1	Slice	Havarti cheese
2	Tablespoon	Tomato sauce
2	Tablespoon	Burger sauce
1	Leaf	Lettuce

Melt dripping in pan on low to medium heat and fry 180 g (6 oz.) burger patty for approximately 8 minutes on each side until cooked through.

Place on round lettuce leaf and add sliced cheese, sliced tomato and diced onion and drizzle with tomato and burger sauce.

Mango pickle curry

This wasn't served at the restaurant but I came up with more recently. My sister described it as one of the best meals she's ever had. Adjust amount of mango pickle to suit, I use twice as much as below.

Serves 6

2	Whole	Carrots
½	Head	Broccoli (or broccolini)
1	Tablespoon	Dripping
1	Large	Onion
1	Whole	Red capsicum (pepper)
300	Grams	Cooked meat (leftover pork)
1	Tin	Whole or diced tomatoes in juice
½	Teaspoon	Salt
2	Tablespoons	Mango pickle
1	Cup	Yogurt
2	Cups	Mashed cauliflower

Make or warm mashed cauliflower. If re-heating mash, fry in small frying pan until heated through and starting to brown.

Bring water to the boil a large saucepan. Peel, top and slice carrot into 3 mm (⅛ in.) slices. Cut broccoli into 2.5 cm (1 in.) florets and stalks. Chop onion and capsicum into 2.5 cm (1 in.) pieces. Boil carrots to soften for 6 minutes, with 2 to 3 minutes to go add broccoli. Strain carrot and broccoli and set aside.

Add dripping to saucepan and fry onion until softened, then add capsicum for 2 minutes stirring occasionally. If whole tomatoes crush into bite-sized pieces by hand and add to saucepan. Add carrots, broccoli, salt, mango pickle and 300 g (10 oz.) cooked meat cut into 1.5 cm (½ in.) pieces. Top with boiling water if not covered and reduce to thicken for 10 to 15 minutes, stirring occasionally.

Make or warm mashed cauliflower. If re-heating mash, fry in small frying pan until heated through and starting to brown.

Serve on bed of hot cauliflower mash with two tablespoons of yogurt.

Salt and pepper squid

This was not an item at the restaurant but the kind of Asian dish I really missed and was quite happy with the taste. I read that the secret to baking squid in the oven is to be really precise about the time. Too little and it's undercooked, too much and it goes rubbery very quickly.

Serves 4

1	Tablespoon	Dripping
500	Grams	Squid
3	Tablespoons	Cauliflower powder
1	Tablespoon	Salt
1	Tablespoon	Pepper, cracked
2	Cups	Mashed cauliflower

Make or heat cauliflower mash. If re-heating mash, fry in small frying pan until heated through and starting to brown.

Place tray in oven and preheat to 190°C (375°F). Cut 500 g (1 lb.) squid tube along edge and dice into 2.5 cm (1 in.) pieces, patting dry if necessary.

Mix salt, pepper and cauliflower powder in strong paper or plastic bag. Add squid in batches appropriate to bag size, maybe two or three batches.

Remove tray from oven and add dripping allowing to melt and place squid on tray evenly distributed. Cook for 9 minutes and then remove tray and turn each piece. Cook for further 9 minutes. Serve on bed of hot cauliflower mash.

Chilli salt and pepper prawns

There was an Asian take-away on the coast that would get my custom every time I visited for the normal version of this dish. I spent some time adjusting every ingredient bit by bit until I was finally happy with the coating mix.

Serves 2

300	Grams	Green prawns (without heads)
1	Handful	Parsley
1	Medium	Onion
1	Whole	Red chilli
1	Tablespoon	Cauliflower powder
½	Teaspoon	Salt
½	Teaspoon	Pepper
¼	Teaspoon	Allspice
1	Pinch	Chilli powder
1	Tablespoon	Dripping

Make or heat cauliflower mash. If re-heating mash, fry in small frying pan until heated through and starting to brown.

Place tray in oven and preheat to 200°C (390°F). Pat dry 300 g (10 oz.) prawns.

Roughly chop parsley. Slice onion and cut slices in half. Halve chilli lengthways, remove seeds and slice.

Mix cauliflower powder, salt, pepper, allspice and chilli powder well in strong paper or plastic bag. Add prawns in batches appropriate to bag size.

Remove tray from oven and add dripping allowing to melt and place prawns on tray. Cook for 5 minutes and then remove tray, turn each piece and add fresh chilli and parsley on top. Cook for a further 5 minutes. Serve on bed of hot cauliflower mash.

Shish tawook

Shish tawooks, grilled marinated chicken kebabs, were the main take away meal my friends and I spent our money on as teenagers. If at all possible try to flame grill. Cooking over a chimenea is perfection.

Serves 6

Marinade

2	Tablespoons	Tomato paste (tin of tomatoes)
½	Cup	Lemon juice
4	Whole	Garlic
5	Tablespoons	Olive oil
3	Tablespoons	Yogurt
3	Tablespoons	Mustard
2	Tablespoons	Apple cider vinegar
2	Teaspoons	Salt
1	Teaspoon	Pepper
1	Teaspoon	Cumin, ground
¾	Teaspoon	Cinnamon
½	Teaspoon	Cardamom, ground
¼	Teaspoon	Turmeric, ground
¼	Teaspoon	Ginger, ground

To make tomato paste puree one tin of tomatoes with stick blender and bring to the boil in a small saucepan. Simmer on low heat stirring occasionally for approximately 1 hour until thickened. Store in refrigerator.

Mince garlic with garlic crush and add all marinade ingredients together and mix well. Cut 1 kg (2 lb.) chicken into 2.5 cm (1 in.) cubes.

Add chicken to marinate and mix ensuring it is covered. Store in air tight container and refrigerate overnight.

Wrap

1	Kilogram	Chicken breast fillet
6	Large	Lettuce leaves
2	Whole	Onions
3	Whole	Tomatoes
1	Teaspoon	Sumac

Cut thin slices of onion and cut in half, rub salt into onion and leave to stand for 10 minutes then rinse with cold water and drain. Add sumac and mix well.

Place marinated chicken cubes on skewers and grill in oven at 180°C (355°F) for 20 minutes.

Check that the chicken is cooked and has no pink in the middle. If possible barbecue or flame grill until chicken is cooked through turning occasionally.

Serve either wrapped in lettuce leaf with sliced tomato and onion or on plate with finely chopped tomato. Can also add tahini sauce and tabouli without the cracked wheat.

Australian kebabs on curry cauliflower rice

This is a basic kebab equivalent with an older Australian flavour. Without a specific sauce it does need pan drippings to give a bit of texture and flavour.

Serves 4

1	Head	Cauliflower
1	Teaspoon	Salt
1	Teaspoon	Turmeric
1	Teaspoon	Sumac
2	Tablespoons	Dripping
1	Large	Onion
400	Grams	Topside steak
4	Rashers	Bacon
1	Large	Onion
1	Whole	Red capsicum (pepper)
1	Whole	Tomato

Place tray or baking dish in oven and preheat to 190°C (375°F). Cut cauliflower into small florets. Mix salt, turmeric and sumac in small container. Remove tray and add 1 tablespoon of dripping, allow to melt then place cauliflower in dish and toss to coat evenly. Sprinkle salt, turmeric and sumac mix over cauliflower and toss again. Place tray in oven and bake for 15 minutes. Remove from oven and allow to cool.

Turn oven down to 180°C (355°F). Cut 400 g (14 oz.) steak into 2.5 cm (1 in.) cubes. Chop bacon, one onion, tomato and capsicum into 2.5 cm (1 in.) pieces. Thread each in turn on to kebab sticks and place on tray. Cook for approximately 30 minutes turning occasionally until cooked through.

Process cooled cauliflower pieces for a few seconds to get them to a rice-like size. Finely dice one onion. In a medium saucepan add 1 tablespoon dripping on a low to medium heat. When dripping is melted add onion and cook stirring regularly until glassy. Add processed cauliflower to onion and stir regularly for a further 2 minutes.

Place kebabs on bed of cauliflower rice and pour pan drippings evenly over.

CHAPTER 4 CONDIMENTS, SAUCES, RUBS, POWDERS & PICKLES

When starting the diet one of the things you realize early on is some time is required making recipes for basic things that are impossible to buy containing legal ingredients. While it does take time you can easily make batches of many of these items that will last for months.

There is a certain sense of empowerment in knowing exactly what is in all your meals and that they contain entirely wholefoods with no bad stuff in them.

I really struggled with mayonnaise early on which frustrated me greatly. After searching for an answer to my problems I finally learnt a few tricks that made it easy. Like many recipes I adjusted the ingredients bit by bit over many batches until I was happy. I made a range of things for a group one day and had one person come up and ask me where I had bought the mayonnaise, as it was the nicest he had ever had. I was pretty chuffed to tell him I made it.

I also never really got into making my own salad dressing even though I knew I should as they just never seemed to taste as good as store bought and I never managed to find an Italian dressing recipe (which was my favorite) that I liked. Now I would never consider buying from the store due to taste alone let alone the cheap oil, sugar and other nasty ingredients they contain.

While it might seem a waste of time I really would encourage people to try dehydrating both celery and cauliflower. They end up being used in a lot of the recipes in here for a reason and it really is not that hard. Think about buying up big on cauliflower when they are in season and nice and cheap as it stores really well too.

Getting into your own pickling is also very worthwhile. That is one thing I have actually done for a long time as it is so easy and pickled and fermented vegetables taste great as well as being great for you, especially when you use apple cider vinegar.

Cauliflower powder

Dehydrating vegetables is actually really easy and you can get a dehydrator quite cheaply these days. For most food types using your oven at the lowest temperature will also work. I tried many different vegetables but the two I liked the most were cauliflower and celery powder. While it will never stick together like wheat flour or cornflour I found cauliflower powder to be great as a coating option, imparting a nice, subtle, unusual flavour. The taste actually goes well with almost any meat.

1	Whole	Cauliflower head

Cut cauliflower into large florets and process briefly. Spread evenly on dehydrator tray.

Dehydrate for 18 hours or until fully dry.

Grind in spice grinder to even powder. Store in covered jar in cool, dark spot.

Celery powder

A lot of the recipes in this book use celery salt made from actual celery powder. I never really liked celery much in recipes as I felt it had too overpowering a taste and I didn't like the texture much either. Celery powder on the other hand gets around the texture problem and has a more subtle, well-balanced taste that is actually really nice.

1	Bunch	Celery

Cut celery into thin slices and spread out evenly on dehydrator tray. Dehydrate for 18 hours or until fully dry.

Grind in spice grinder to even powder. Store in covered jar in cool, dark spot.

Celery salt

While it can easily be bought most commercial brands of celery salt include rice flour and can include oils and worst of all undesirable anti-caking agents. Early on I started making and mixing my own celery salt made from real celery and thought it was much better.

155	Grams	Salt (68%)
54	Grams	Celery powder (24%)
9	Grams	Paprika, ground (4%)
9	Grams	Parsley, dried (4%)

Weigh out 155 g (5½ oz.) of salt, 54 g (2 oz.) of celery powder, 9 g (⅓ oz.) of paprika and 9 g (⅓ oz.) of parsley and combine in jar twice the size and shake well, transfer into appropriate sized jar.

Roast chicken rub

This chicken rub approaches that of the main fried chicken take-away. It isn't the same but very nice.

12	Teaspoons	Salt
4	Teaspoons	Pepper
4	Teaspoons	Celery salt
4	Teaspoons	Garlic powder
4	Teaspoons	Paprika, ground
4	Teaspoons	Onion powder
4	Teaspoons	Thyme, dried
4	Teaspoons	Basil, dried
4	Teaspoons	Oregano, dried

Add each component to large jar and shake well, transfer into appropriate sized jar for contents.

Chicken fillet coating

I tried many different mixes for a coating for chicken fillets sometimes with a large list of ingredients and then worked back to just keeping the ones I thought most important and actually found it better.

4	Tablespoons	Cauliflower powder
4	Teaspoons	Salt
4	Teaspoons	Pepper
4	Teaspoons	Celery salt

Add each component to large jar and shake well, transfer into appropriate sized jar for contents.

Gravy (onion)

This provides a tasty and somewhat thickened gravy. It also makes a handy base for a number of recipes requiring gravy and cooked onion.

Serves 4

1	Cup	Chicken drippings
½	Teaspoon	Salt
1	Large	Onion

Bake skinned onion (with roast chicken) for 45 minutes. Place onion in container, add water to half cover and puree with stick blender to smooth consistency. Add to small saucepan on low heat.

Collect pan drippings from roast chicken when cooked and add to saucepan and stir for 3 minutes to combine. Add salt to taste.

Gravy (mayo)

An alternative to using onion is to use mayonnaise to slightly thicken gravy. This is very tasty but re-heating is a bit problematic.

Serves 4

1	Cup	Chicken drippings
3	Tablespoons	Mayonnaise
½	Teaspoon	Salt

Pour pan drippings from roast chicken into small mixing bowl. Add mayonnaise and salt and stir well.

Do not cook mayonnaise (egg). If re-heating heat on lowest setting very slowly.

Curry powder

I found many curry powders had the chance of containing or being contaminated with gluten and so just made my own instead, it's really not that hard and again you know exactly what is in it.

2	Tablespoons	Cumin, ground
2	Tablespoons	Coriander, ground
2	Teaspoons	Turmeric, ground
½	Teaspoon	Cayenne pepper
½	Teaspoon	Mustard, ground
½	Teaspoon	Ginger, ground
½	Teaspoon	Fenugreek, ground
½	Teaspoon	Celery powder

Add each component to large jar and shake well, transfer into appropriate sized jar for contents.

Garam masala

A lot of mixed spices can contain rice flour or be contaminated with gluten. If you cannot find a decent garam masala you can make your own using the powdered forms of each ingredient. If you get more adventurous buy the ingredients as whole seeds and toast them for a few minutes on a frying pan and use a spice grinder to make a fine powder. The flavour is much better again.

38	Grams	Pepper (25%)
35	Grams	Caraway (23%)
29	Grams	Fennel (19%)
21	Grams	Cardamom (14%)
15	Grams	Cinnamon (10%)
14	Grams	Cloves (9%)

Weigh out 38 g (1⅓ oz.) of pepper, 35 g (1¼ oz.) of caraway, 29 g (1 oz.) of fennel, 21 g (¾ oz.) of cardamom, 15 g (½ oz.) of cinnamon and 14 g (½ oz.) of cloves and combine in a jar twice the size and shake well. Transfer into appropriate sized jar.

Chicken stock

I strongly believe this is the most nutritious food you can have and an absolutely essential requirement to healing. There's a reason our ancestors always recommended having chicken soup if you were sick. I am quite sure if you have meat stock-based soup every day you will significantly reduce the amount of colds and flu you get. That is it is your immune system's best friend. I also really pay attention to what my body (gut) tells me after I eat a meal now and it is always very happy after soup.

Serves 2 litres

2	Litres	Water
1	Whole	Leftover bones from roast chicken (or whole chicken)
1	Large	Onion
1	Large	Carrot
1	Stem	Celery
3	Sprigs	Thyme, fresh
1	Handful	Parsley, fresh
1	Teaspoon	Salt
¼	Cup	Apple cider vinegar

Add meat bones to large pot and fill to ¾ full with approximately 2 litres (4½ lb.) water.

Roughly chop onion, carrot and celery and add to pot. Add salt, apple cider vinegar, thyme and parsley.

Cover pot with lid and bring to the boil then turn down to simmer. Simmer stirring occasionally for 8 hours.

Strain and pour into appropriate covered container, preferably glass. Store in refrigerator.

Worcestershire sauce

This I use just for adding to cottage pie. It is another one where you have lost a number of the main ingredients and it is not nice and thick but I don't feel you lose too much in the taste, especially when it is an ingredient for a dish.

Serves 1 Cup

1	Cup	Apple cider vinegar
1	Teaspoon	Pepper
1	Teaspoon	Onion powder
1	Teaspoon	Garlic powder
½	Teaspoon	Ginger, ground
½	Teaspoon	Chilli powder
¼	Teaspoon	Cloves, ground
¼	Teaspoon	Cinnamon

Add all ingredients to a small saucepan on a medium heat and bring to the boil stirring occasionally.

Simmer for 2 minutes and pour into covered glass container suitable for pouring.

Italian salad dressing

This dressing is adapted from a recipe by Nealey Dozier from The Kitchn dot com and has completely converted me from ever buying salad dressing again.

Serves 10

½	Cup	Apple cider vinegar
½	Teaspoon	Honey
1	Whole	Green onion (shallot)
1	Clove	Garlic
1	Tablespoon	Red capsicum (pepper)
1	Cup	Olive oil
1	Teaspoon	Mustard
1	Teaspoon	Salt
¼	Teaspoon	Pepper
¼	Teaspoon	Chilli flakes
¼	Teaspoon	Oregano, dried
¼	Teaspoon	Marjoram, dried

Heat vinegar and honey in small saucepan on lowest heat. Once honey has melted remove from heat and stir.

Finely chop shallots. Mince garlic and capsicum using garlic press removing skins.

Using an approximately 400 ml (14 oz.) glass jar add olive oil, shallots, garlic, capsicum, mustard, salt, pepper, chilli flakes, oregano and marjoram. Place lid on jar and shake well.

Store in refrigerator. Preferably leave for two days for flavours to develop. Shake well before each use.

Mustard

In truth I have never been 100% happy with mustard outcomes but as it is mostly used as an ingredient within other recipes it does the job nicely while avoiding all the bad things found in commercial mustard.

¾	Cup	**Mustard seeds**
1	Cup	**Water**
½	Teaspoon	**Turmeric, ground**
¼	Teaspoon	**Salt**
1	Dash	**Garlic powder**
1	Dash	**Paprika, ground**
½	Cup	**Apple cider vinegar**

Grind mustard seeds to powder in spice grinder. Add water, mustard, turmeric, salt, garlic powder and paprika to a small saucepan and bring to the boil.

Simmer for 30 to 40 minutes stirring occasionally.

Take off stove and whisk vinegar into mix. Pour into covered glass container and leave on bench overnight and then refrigerate.

Tomato sauce

This sauce is adapted from a recipe from Paleo Leap. Initially I assessed a number of recipes for tomato sauce most of which made it entirely from scratch. It really seemed the bulk of the work was in preparing the tomatoes so when I realised you could simply use a can of tomatoes I was quite happy and it really isn't that difficult.

Serves 15

400	Grams	Tinned tomatoes
2	Tablespoons	Apple cider vinegar
1	Teaspoon	Honey
½	Teaspoon	Onion powder
½	Teaspoon	Cinnamon
¼	Teaspoon	Mustard powder
¼	Teaspoon	Salt
1	Pinch	Cloves, ground
1	Pinch	Allspice

Puree one tin (1 lb.) of tomatoes with stick blender and add to small saucepan slowly bringing to the boil.

Simmer for 45 minutes scraping down sides and stirring occasionally.

Add vinegar, honey, onion powder, cinnamon, mustard powder, salt, cloves and allspice and simmer for 5 minutes or until achieving a thickness you prefer. Store in refrigerator in covered glass container.

Mayonnaise

*I really struggled with mayonnaise at the beginning until I discovered that water is the enemy of emulsification. Once I started adding the wet ingredients at the end and concentrating on pouring the first ¼ cup of oil **really** slowly it was easy. I then played around with all the ingredients for some time and was finally very happy with the outcome. I actually quite like using grapeseed oil but it is very hard to source cold pressed and has a high proportion of polyunsaturated fat unfortunately. At the restaurant we only used macadamia oil but did try a number of the cold pressed brands until we found one that was light in flavour where the macadamia did not over-power the taste. I think the company actually developed that blend specifically for mayonnaise.*

1	Cup	Macadamia oil
1	Whole	Egg
½	Teaspoon	Salt
¼	Teaspoon	Pepper
2	Teaspoons	Apple cider vinegar
2	Teaspoons	Lemon juice
½	Teaspoon	Mustard
½	Teaspoon	Honey

Place egg, salt and freshly cracked pepper into deep container and mix using stick blender for a few seconds. Very, very slowly add first ¼ cup of macadamia oil blending continuously. Pour the first quarter cup of oil in as slowly as you can in a continuous drizzle.

Once well-emulsified continue to add remaining oil while blending.

Add vinegar, lemon juice, mustard and honey and blend until combined.

Add additional salt, pepper, lemon juice or vinegar to taste. Be careful with the amount of apple cider vinegar as some can overpower the taste very quickly. In this case use less vinegar and more lemon juice.

Tartare sauce

If I know I want some tartare sauce with a fish meal I usually don't make a whole batch as below but just take the amount I need from an existing batch of mayonnaise and cut down the proportion of ingredients accordingly. Leave overnight at least to allow the flavours to blend and mellow.

1	Cup	Mayonnaise
2	Whole	Gherkins
1	Whole	Green onion (shallot)
1	Tablespoon	Capers
1	Tablespoon	Parsley, fresh
2	Teaspoons	Lemon rind
2	Teaspoons	Lemon juice
¼	Teaspoon	Salt

Finely chop gherkins, capers, shallot and parsley and add to mayonnaise in small mixing bowl. Add lemon rind and juice and salt and mix well.

Leave in refrigerator overnight to blend.

Garlic sauce

This is effectively a strong garlic mayonnaise but only using egg whites, it goes nicely with shish tawooks or used instead of mayonnaise for the chicken fillet wrap. It is also used as a dipping sauce for almost any vegetable or meat.

5	Cloves	Garlic
⅔	Teaspoon	Salt
1	Whole	Egg
1	Cup	Avocado or macadamia oil
4	Teaspoons	Lemon juice

Peel garlic and add to a deep container with salt. Mix using stick blender to make a paste as much as possible. Separate and add egg white only and blend for 3 seconds. Very slowly add first ¼ cup of oil blending continuously. Pour the first quarter cup of oil in as slowly as you can. The mix should thicken up so oil sits on the top. Continue to add remaining oil while blending. Add lemon juice until combined.

Burger sauce

This is a simple mayonnaise-based sauce we used for the burger wrap and burger stack. Make sure it is made the day before so the onion blends in.

1	Cup	Mayonnaise
4	Tablespoons	Italian salad dressing
3	Tablespoons	Gherkins
2	Tablespoons	Onion
2	Teaspoons	Apple cider vinegar
1	Teaspoon	Honey
½	Teaspoon	Salt

Finely dice onion and gherkins. Combine all ingredients and stir. Refrigerate overnight to allow flavours to develop and onion to mellow.

Pickled garlic

Pickled garlic makes a great snack and also provides a good emergency source of garlic should you find yourself short. It is mainly included in here as it is an ingredient of the Austrian potato salad. Really makes a difference too.

3	Bulbs	Garlic
1	Cup	Apple cider vinegar
½	Tablespoon	Salt
4	Leaves	Basil, fresh
5	Whole	Cloves

Peel garlic. Sterilise a glass jar that fits them with a little space left over with boiling water. Add same amount of vinegar as jar contains to a small saucepan on low heat and slowly bring to boil. Add salt at a rate of ½ tablespoon per cup vinegar.

Once brine has come to a light boil add garlic cloves and simmer for 3 minutes. Add cloves and basil to bottom of jar and then scoop garlic in and cover with brine mix. If short of liquid to fill add boiling water.

Store in a cool dark area. Can be eaten after 3 days. Refrigerate after opening.

Pickled banana (or sweet) chilli

My sister first started pickling banana chilli after we got into the habit of buying commercial ones and then whole banana chilli started becoming readily available in shops for the first time. We used to use malt vinegar but when I had to switch to apple cider vinegar I actually decided I preferred it. Goes very well with cheese, especially Havarti, and some Kalamata olives as a nice end of day snack.

Serves 12

10	Whole	Banana chillies
2	Cups	Apple cider vinegar
1	Tablespoon	Salt
8	Leaves	Basil, fresh
10	Whole	Cloves

Cut off banana chilli tops (with seeds) and halve them both length and crosswise removing seeds.

Sterilise a glass jar that fits them with a little space left over with boiling water. Add same amount of vinegar as jar contains to a small to medium saucepan on low heat and slowly bring to boil. Add salt at a rate of ½ tablespoon per cup vinegar.

Add cloves and basil to bottom of jar and then add chilli packing them in tightly if possible.

Once brine has come to a light boil cover chilli with brine mix. If short of liquid to fill add boiling water. Store in a cool dark area. Leave at least 5 days. Refrigerate after opening.

Mango pickle

Mango pickle is the absolutely essential ingredient for the mango pickle curry. While it is easy to obtain commercially a lot of the ingredients are not gut friendly. It isn't difficult to make but does need to be made ahead of time and the sourcing of green mangos can be difficult.

1	Whole	Green mango
2	Tablespoons	Chilli powder
1	Tablespoon	Mustard powder
1	Teaspoon	Turmeric, ground
2	Teaspoons	Salt
1	Teaspoon	Fenugreek
1	Teaspoon	Onion powder
¼	Cup	Mustard seed oil, cold pressed

Wash mango and pat dry with paper towel. Chop mango with skin included into 2 cm (¾ in.) sized pieces and add spices and oil and mix. Leave covered for 2 days. Stir well.

CHAPTER 5 DESSERTS

My main aim with desserts was to make a treat that could be had for morning or afternoon tea using as little sugar as possible.

As a lot of the guidance on these diets advises just because honey and dates are tolerated does not mean you should have them in large amounts. I also agree with those that say you should not have more than ¼ cup almond flour a day. To occasionally have a little more as a treat is fine but not all the time.

The downsides of almond flour is it has to be watched carefully when baking as it can start to burn very quickly and of course it does not stick together or rise like wheat flour. The upside is it has a much nicer taste and you can use significantly less sugar to achieve a good outcome. I actually prefer almond flour pastry to normal pastry, more expensive and you have to be careful in the handling but it leads to a really tasty pastry.

I always thought my desserts were an acceptable alternative to normal equivalents but would not compete that well in taste if you did not care what you ate. I am still surprised at how many people seem to really like them though. Perhaps it is in part because they subconsciously realize they do not feel sick afterwards.

Our best-selling dessert was the almond mini donuts. They got off to a slow start I think because they looked a bit strange but were a definite favorite of staff and eventually customers too. The carrot cake muffins with and without lemon butter icing sold consistently well from start to finish.

If you trying to lose weight I would recommend sticking to carrot cake muffins as much as possible, they really do seem to be fat storage neutral, especially (and no one believes me on this but I experimented a number of times always with the same outcome) if you include having them with butter. I do not know why but my theory is that the increased fat proportion reduces the relative proportion of sugar that bit more so that when consumed at the same time it does not push the body into deciding to store the sugar away as body fat.

Another tip I would give to people who like something sweet and comforting after dinner is to just have a teaspoon of peanut butter instead of reaching for chocolate or something similar.

Once I was better I experimented a lot on weight loss and gain using varying amounts of exercise and sugar and starch. In the end I came to the conclusion that exercise is definitely the lesser part of the equation. Good for fitness but I estimated only 20% of the equation to losing weight, the amount of sugar and starch you eat making up 80%.

When I first got into low carbohydrate eating I remember one of the early books suggested not to eat more than the equivalent of six slices of bread in total starch and sugar per week.

From my experiments I believe this is about right. Once you go over this amount your body goes into fat storage mode, but if you can keep under it most of the time weight loss and maintenance is really easy.

Almond mini donuts

This was our top selling dessert despite a slow start. At first we made them using a pop cake maker as small balls, where I think they were just too unusual looking. After the first month or so we bought a mini donut maker and it was surprising the difference the shape made in appealing to customers. Later on we also sold them heated with a lemon sauce and dollop of French cream gelato which quickly became a favourite of a number of our regulars.

Serves 20

60	Grams	Butter
1	Cup	Almond flour
1	Teaspoon	Cinnamon
¼	Teaspoon	Bicarbonate of soda
¼	Teaspoon	Salt
2	Whole	Eggs (two small to medium or one large)
2	Tablespoons	Honey
1	Teaspoon	Vanilla extract

Requires mini donut maker or pop cake maker.

Melt 60 g (2 oz.) butter in small saucepan on low heat. Combine almond flour, salt, bicarbonate of soda and cinnamon in medium sized bowl and mix well.

Once butter is melted remove a small amount to coat donut maker using heat proof pastry brush to coat both sides.

Add honey to butter until melted and stir.

In a small mixing bowl combine eggs and vanilla and lightly whisk. Add eggs and butter mix to dry ingredients and mix well with spoon. Immediately spoon into donut maker.

Ready when golden brown.

If serving immediately roll donuts in leftover honey and butter mix with a light dusting of cinnamon.

Carrot cake muffin

This is my regular tea time dessert. They fill the desire (habit) to have a treat with a hot drink for morning and afternoon tea and are really low in sugar. It was a recipe where I was really aiming to see how low I could go with sugar content and still have something with an appealing taste. For me it was an acceptable substitute to a normal sugar-laden muffin so I continue to be surprised by how many people say they really like them. I always make a large batch and freeze half of them as they freeze and defrost really well.

Serves 12

¼	Cup	Almonds (optional)
2	Cups	Carrots
3	Cups	Almond flour
4	Teaspoons	Cinnamon
2	Teaspoon	Mace (or Nutmeg)
1	Teaspoon	Bicarbonate of soda
½	Teaspoon	Salt
4	Whole	Eggs
½	Cup	Macadamia oil
2	Teaspoons	Vanilla extract
½	Cup	Honey

Crush or finely chop almonds to small pieces. Peel, top and grate carrots.

In a large mixing bowl combine almond flour, cinnamon, mace, bicarbonate of soda and salt and mix well.

In a small mixing bowl lightly whisk eggs and add oil and vanilla.

Add carrot to dry ingredients and mix with a spoon. Add egg mix and honey to dry ingredients and combine. Add chopped nuts and mix well.

Scoop mix into muffin trays to ¾ full and bake at 170°C (340°F) for 30 to 40 minutes.

Watch after 30 minutes for burning and test with toothpick. A little dry and slightly browned is better than undercooked.

Top with butter or lemon butter icing on next page.

Lemon butter icing

There was some disagreement for this recipe with cooks and staff. I was as always aiming for a minimum use of sugar yet something that lifted the taste ever so slightly sugar-wise. Because of that I used a minimum of lemon juice and eventually greater amounts of zest to juice to give it a light lemony taste without needing extra honey and without making it sour and detracting from the already low sugar content of the muffin. I was well and truly out voted though. This is the original recipe but if you are apparently like the majority of people you may want to add more lemon juice.

Serves 6

125	Grams	Butter
1	Tablespoon	Honey
1	Teaspoon	Lemon zest
1	Teaspoon	Lemon juice

Beat 125 g (4½ oz.) of butter to cream, add honey and lemon juice and zest and beat until well combined and butter is soft and light in colour.

Honey butter sauce

This is the fancy or more decadent sauce option I use with carrot cake muffins but you heat them and add a warm honey butter sauce and French cream mix like sticky date pudding but without all the sugar.

Serves 6

250	Grams	Butter
½	Cup	Honey
1	Cup	French cream mix

Add 250 g (9 oz.) butter and honey to a small saucepan on a low heat and simmer for 5 minutes stirring frequently.

Warm muffins in oven at 150°C (300°F) for 10 minutes. Top muffins with honey butter sauce and dollop of French cream mix.

French cream mix/gelato

I spent a lot of time trying to come up with a dairy free ice cream using almond milk. Despite much effort I never felt any of the results were suitable for sale. They were probably OK if you couldn't have any dairy and had no choice but I was quite sure no one who could have dairy would ever have ordered it twice.

I think it was around this time that Crème fraiche became readily available at the shops so I decided to try it out as an option and was much happier.

Making your own long-fermented crème fraiche is also really easy, it might require ordering the special mix of bacterial starter from your health food store but otherwise is exactly the same process as making yogurt except you use cream instead of milk. Crème fraiche is different to sour cream, it has some different textual and heating and cooking properties and also a really nice ever so slightly lemony flavour.

Serves 12

2	Cups	Crème fraiche
3	Tablespoons	Honey
2	Teaspoons	Vanilla extract

Heat crème fraiche and honey on very low heat in small saucepan until honey has melted and combined. Add vanilla and mix well with whisk.

Refrigerate in covered container to harden overnight.

This makes a simple sweetened French cream mix that can be added to desserts and used in tarts.

To make gelato place cooled mix in gelato or ice cream maker for specified time.

French cream tart

The first time I tasted the French cream gelato mix just prior to popping it into the machine (after cooling and thickening in the fridge) I felt I had a viable option for making an individual cheesecake like alternative. I made an almond flour pastry to form a tart. I was really surprised at how nice almond flour pastry is. I always have to make extra pastry as despite my best intentions it is inevitably really badly nibbled in its raw state before it makes it to the tray. I do think even long-fermented cream should be avoided as much as possible though and this was only ever an occasional treat later in the diet. If fruit is tolerated they are also nice topped with stewed apricot.

Serves 12

350	Grams	Almond flour
90	Grams	Butter
2	Tablespoons	Honey
½	Teaspoon	Salt
¼	Teaspoon	Bicarbonate of soda
2	Cups	French cream mix

Place large square of cling wrap on counter. Add 350 g (12 oz.) almond flour into a large mixing bowl. Cut 90 g (3 oz.) of butter into pieces into bowl and mix together with hands until it becomes a single ball. Add honey and mix well. Wrap ball in cling wrap and rest in refrigerator for 45 minutes.

Preheat oven to 150°C (300°F). Place large sheet of baking paper on counter and remove ball from cling wrap and fold one side of baking paper over ball. Flatten with hands and roll out with rolling pin to 2 to 3 mm (⅛ in.) thin. Use pastry cutter or thin edged glass to cut round pieces slightly larger than muffin tray base and gently place them in tray pushing them into edges. Extra may be required to build up sides.

Bake for 10 minutes until light brown. Allow to cool in tray and then place muffin tray in refrigerator to harden. Remove tart casings gently after 1 hour and keep stored in refrigerator until use.

Fill tart casings with French cream mix when ready to serve (casings will become soggy and fall apart when handling within a few hours of adding filling).

Cacao date balls

There are loads of date or protein ball recipes around now. Where I like these is using the cacao butter, it ups the fat content nicely and makes for a pleasing combination of fat and sugar. They are a good alternative to chocolate. It's not really the same but does the trick.

Serves 20

115	**Grams**	**Cacao butter**
1	**Cup**	**Sesame seeds**
1	**Cup**	**Sunflower seeds**
2	**Cups**	**Dates**

Slowly heat 115 g (4 oz.) cacao butter in small saucepan on low heat.

Process sesame seeds to flour consistency and add to large mixing bowl. Then process sunflower seeds to flour consistency and add to bowl.

Process dates for approximately 60 seconds until they are sticky but not quite sticking together in one big lump. Add seeds back into processor with dates and process until combined for about 20 seconds.

Transfer to a large bowl and add melted cacao butter and mix well with hands. Massage into 2.5 cm (1 in.) balls and place on plate to cool in refrigerator for an hour then store in a covered container either on counter or in refrigerator.

CHAPTER 6 DRINKS

One of the easiest ways to consume high amounts of sugar and increase fat storage is to drink soft drinks, fruit juice, sports drinks or flavored milk drinks. These drinks generally contain 10% sugar or some 10 to 20 teaspoons per serving if not more.

A simple and vastly better alternative is to make a fresh fruit juice spritzer. Even better is to avoid the fruit and have a ginger spritzer either with a small amount of honey or better yet none at all.

For me it took some time to realize that even small amounts of fruit would result in quite marked abdominal distension. I did feel that once I stopped eating fruit my final healing took off.

I found the only forms of sugar I could tolerate were dates and honey. I still do not know why dates were acceptable and all other fruit not.

I would always suggest that keeping to room temperature chlorine-free water is by far the best way to go.

A ginger spritzer makes for a refreshing and healthy choice occasionally. Peppermint tea is also a great alternative to tea or coffee. I found the chai peppermint tea to be a really nice drink later in the day if you feel like something more interesting and especially if avoiding caffeine altogether.

Fruit juice, even spritzers, almond milk smoothies, caffeine and alcohol should all be had as occasional treats and later in the diet.

I will never be convinced that coffee is good for you. What you experience when you have stayed off it for several months and then have one should convince you too. I think once you are better there is no problem having one occasionally but I do not think several times a day is a good idea and certainly not when you are trying to heal.

I believe tea is much more benign in general however I have wondered whether it does something undesirable in regards to mouth microfauna composition.

Grape juice spritzer

The grape and ginger spritzers were by far the best sellers. It was quite a surprise that the ginger drinks and in fact the no sugar ginger drink was the best seller. The grape spritzer was definitely the favourite of younger people though.

Serves 10

1	**Bag**	**Grapes (Midnight beauty)**

Depending on what equipment you have different methods can be used. A cold press juicer is best or otherwise a blender. Press grapes according to directions of the juicer. Alternatively use a blender and then a nut bag to strain. If blending it is recommended to remove the grapes from the stems first.

Add 40 ml (1½ oz.) grape juice to 1 cup of sparkling mineral water or soda water and stir.

Apple juice spritzer

The apple spritzer is cheap and easy to source year round but never sold as well as the other spritzers because of the brown unappealing colour it goes quite quickly as it oxidises. You can add lemon juice to prevent this from happening but I always felt that was a worse option as you are then dulling the sweetened taste and require more sugar to compensate. Putting it in a coloured container works well.

Serves 8

10	**Whole**	**Apples (red delicious, gala, pink lady)**

Depending on what equipment you have different methods can be used. A cold press juicer is best or otherwise a blender. If using a cold press juicer quarter or eighth cut apples and press. Alternatively use a blender and peel, core and quarter cut the apples and place in blender. Depending on the blender you may need to add a small amount (¼ cup) of water to make it blend properly. Use a nut bag to strain.

Add 70 ml (2½ oz.) apple juice to 1 cup of sparkling mineral water or soda water and stir.

Blood orange juice spritzer

If you are more advanced into the diet and feel you must have a small amount of alcohol this with a potato based vodka is quite nice. I called it a 'Pen-driver'.

Serves 8

10	**Whole**	**Blood oranges**

Squeeze oranges and strain if required.
Add 90 ml (3 oz.) orange juice to 1 cup of sparkling mineral water or soda water and stir.

Almond milk

Blanched almonds will give a smoother consistency but you may want to look into what chemicals are used to blanch almonds before making that decision.

Serves 3 cups

3	**Cups**	**Water**
1	**Cup**	**Almonds (blanched or whole)**

Soak almonds for 12 hours (overnight) in water that covers them and then a bit more. Once soaked strain and rinse almonds under running water. Depending on what equipment you have different methods can be used. Preferably use a cold press juicer adding the water as per instructions and use a nut bag to do a final fine strain.

Alternatively use a blender adding almonds and water and then nut bag to strain.

Ginger spider

A large part of the idea of the restaurant was to provide people, and especially children (whether they were dealing with gut issues or food intolerances), with a place where they could feel normal and not deprived while valiantly doing the right thing for their gut or avoiding what they were unlucky enough to have to avoid. We tried to provide as large a range of better alternatives as possible including an ice cream float option.

Serves 1

1	Scoop	French cream gelato
2	Tablespoons	Honey ginger mix
1	Cup	Soda water

Add two tablespoons of soda water to the glass followed by the gelato ball, then pour ginger syrup over gelato, top up with soda water and stir.

Banana smoothie

This was definitely a favourite with staff, even those who had no problem with milk. I would suggest it is no more than a once a week treat though.

Serves 1

1	Cup	Almond milk
1	Whole	Banana
¼	Cup	Ice
½	Teaspoon	Vanilla extract
1	Dash	Cinnamon
1	Teaspoon	Honey

Add almond milk, cut banana and ice, cinnamon and vanilla extract. At very end add honey and immediately blend.

Ginger spritzer (plain) mix

This is my favourite drink, no sugar but very refreshing. I do not think it should be had every day though. I would usually make a batch once every month or so that would last a week. You can also freeze them as ice cubes to have ready but they are not as good as fresh.
Serves 8

1	Cup	Water
4	Tablespoons	Ginger

Finely grate ginger. Add water to a small saucepan on low to medium heat and bring to a light boil. Add ginger and simmer on low heat for 10 minutes stirring occasionally.

Take saucepan off heat and steep for 45 minutes. Strain with tea strainer or fine strainer into pourable glass container and store in refrigerator. Keeps for approximately 1 week.

Add two tablespoons ginger mix to 1 cup of sparkling mineral water or soda water with a slice of lemon.

Ginger spritzer with honey mix

If you prefer the sweetened version of the ginger spritzer mix try using half or even less the honey to see what amount you like. I like to keep the leftover pulp to use in various stir fry recipes such as the chicken garam masala.
Serves 8

1	Cup	Water
4	Tablespoons	Ginger
4	Tablespoons	Honey

Use the same process as for the plain ginger spritzer adding honey as well as ginger.

Add two tablespoons of honey ginger mix to 1 cup of sparkling mineral water or soda water.

Chai mix

This is a basic and easy to make chai recipe that includes the main ingredients of chai, which can take numerous forms.

Serves 4

1	Cup	Water
4	Tablespoons	Ginger
¼	Teaspoon	Cinnamon
¼	Teaspoon	Nutmeg
1	Dash	Allspice

Finely grate ginger. On low to medium heat in a small saucepan bring water to a light boil and add ginger, cinnamon, nutmeg and allspice and simmer on low heat for 10 minutes stirring occasionally. Take off heat and steep in saucepan for 45 minutes. Strain with tea strainer or fine strainer into pourable glass container and store in refrigerator. Keeps for approximately 1 week.

Chai peppermint tea

Every now and then I would have completely caffeine and/or sugar free weeks. I found this a great drink at those times or at night when you feel like a more interesting hot drink but know that caffeine will interrupt your sleep.

Serves 1

2	Tablespoons	Chai mix
1	Cup	Water
1	Bag	Peppermint tea bag

Add chai mix to boiling water with peppermint tea bag, leave too steep for at least 5 minutes. Adjust amount of chai mix to taste.

Almond chai

There was one otherwise pretty quiet male customer who told us this was the best chai latte he had ever had. It was also a favourite of a number of the cooks especially later in the day. What we did find with the staff though was that the amount of chai mix was very individual, some of us liked just a tablespoon or two of chai while others preferred an almost half and half mix.

Serves 1

1	**Cup**	**Almond milk**
¼	**Cup**	**Chai mix**

Add chai mix to heated almond milk, add honey to taste.

ABOUT THE AUTHOR

Penelope Baalman is a forest scientist (forester) who works in the area of climate change mitigation. She has had a strong interest in the use of food for health since 2002 when following dental disease she was introduced to the work of Weston A. Price. Her main current interest is in the function of the gastrointestinal and immune systems and their effect on mental health. She lives on the north coast of New South Wales, Australia.

30837491R00066

Printed in Great Britain
by Amazon